Growing Bulbs

WRITER

Barbara Ferguson Stremple

PHOTOGRAPHER

Saxon Holt

LAWN & GARDEN

Product Manager: CYNTHIA FOLLAND, NK LAWN & GARDEN CO.

Acquisition, Development and Production Services:
JENNINGS & KEEFE: Media Development, Corte Madera, CA

Acquisition: JACK JENNINGS, BOB DOLEZAL

Series Concept: BOB DOLEZAL

Project Director: JILL FOX

Developmental Editor: CYNTHIA PUTNAM

Horticultural Consultant: RG TURNER JR

Photographic Director: SAXON HOLT

Art Director (interior): BRAD GREENE

Cover Designer: KAREN EMERSON

Page Make-up: BRAD GREENE

Illustrator: JAMES BALKOVEK

Copy Editor: VIRGINIA RICH

Proofreader: LYNN FERAR

Indexer: SYLVIA COATES

Photo Assistant: PEGGY HENRY

Additional Photographers: Pages 6-7 (background) and 27 (Double-Digging) Alan Copeland and Barry Shapiro; pages 32-33 (Botrytis, Borers, Thrips and Viruses) Margery Daughtrey; pages 54 (Amaryllis), 57 (Cape hyacinth), 59 (Foxtail lily), 61 (Glory-of-the-snow), 65 (Candidum hybrids), 70 (Puschkinia and Snowdrop), 71 (Squill) and 75 (Winter aconite) Netherlands Flowerbulb Information Center; pages 67 (Montbretia) and 71 (Spider lily) Charles Cresson

Color Separations: PREPRESS ASSEMBLY INCORPORATED

Printing and Binding: WOLFER PRINTING COMPANY

PRINTED IN THE USA

Cover: Perky candy-stripped tulips provide early spring color along an entrance path.

95   96   97   10   9   8   7   6   5   4   3   2   1

First Edition

Library of Congress Cataloging-in-Publication Data:
Stremple, Barbara Ferguson.
    Growing bulbs / writer, Barbara Ferguson Stremple : photographer, Saxon Holt.
      p. cm.
    Includes index.
    ISBN 1-880281-16-3 (paper)
    1. Bulbs.   I. Holt, Saxon.   II. Title.
SB425.S87 1994
635.9' 44 -- dc20   94-34535
                                                  CIP

Special thanks to: Brookside Botanic Garden, Montgomery, MD; Valerie Brown; Theo Crawford; Margery Daughtrey, Cornell University, Ithaca, NY; Dan Davids, Davids & Royston Bulbs, Gardena, CA; Phil Edinger; Sally Ferguson, Netherlands Flowerbulb Information Center; Filoli Gardens, Woodside, CA; Peggy Henry; Longwood Gardens, Kennett Square, PA; Star MacKay; Dorothy Orr; Beth Records; Wayne Roderick; Diana Stratton; Katie Trefethen; Debbie Van Bourgondlen, Van Bourgondlen Bulbs, Babylon, NY

TABLE OF CONTENTS

Enjoying Bulbs 4–5
Five Bulb Gardens 6–7
Types of Bulbs 8–9
The Bulb Life Cycle 10–11
Hardy Versus Tender Bulbs 12–13
Bulbs for All Seasons 14–15
Designing the Garden 16–17
Companion Planting 18–19
Planting Depths & Growing Heights 20–23
Choosing Bulbs 24–25
Preparing to Plant 26–27
Planting Bulbs 28–29
Year-round Bulb Care 30–31
Controlling Pests & Diseases 32–33
End-of-Season Care 34–35
Dividing Bulbs 36–37
Letting Bulbs Naturalize 38–39
Bulbs for Shady Places 40–41
Bulbs for Fragrance 42–43
Bulbs for Cutting 44–45
Bulbs for Outdoor Containers 46–47
Easy Indoor Bulbs 48–49
Out-of-Season Blooming 50–51
Bulb Data Chart 52–53
Bulb Gallery 54–75
Planting Zone Map 76–77
Index 78–79
A Note from NK Lawn & Garden 80

ENJOYING BULBS

WHY GROW BULBS?

Planting a bulb is like hiding a secret treasure. You bury it in the ground, see nothing for months and often forget all about it. Then one day a small green sprout appears, signaling the arrival of a new season. The sprout matures into a wonderful flower of any imaginable color, blooms radiantly and then slowly retreats underground into dormancy until the cycle begins again the following season.

Bulbs are unique in the flower garden. They require very little care and yet produce some of the showiest flowers in nature. There are bulbs that thrive in the coldest or the warmest of climates. Unlike perennials, they need little or no pruning, staking or transplanting, and unlike annuals, most come back every year. They take up little space and can enliven any garden.

Most bulbs bloom in the spring, and many people think of flowering bulbs as a sign of spring, but there are bulbs that bloom in every season of the year. Winter aconite, *Eranthis hyemalis,* grows right up through the snow in late winter or early spring, exploding with bright yellow blossoms that resemble buttercups and carry a sweet, honey fragrance. There are many summer-blooming bulbs and quite a few fall-blooming bulbs as well. Although they may be less noticeable than spring bulbs because of the other plants flowering around them, they too can be added to many gardens for nearly year-round bulb beauty.

BULBS IN NATURE

Knowing the origin of a bulb gives you clues to its requirements. Of the bulbs we grow today, many of the spring-flowering bulbs originated in the Mediterranean region, from Spain and North Africa across into Turkey, and in Iran and western China. Those regions have wet winters and hot, dry summers, so the bulbs have adapted by beginning growth in winter and flowering in the cool, wet spring. During its growing period, the plant stores food in the underground bulb, and then, as summer heat and drought approach, the plant dies back.

Summer-flowering bulbs typically come from parts of Africa where the wet and dry cycles are different from those of the Mediterranean region. The rain occurs in the hot months, and the winters are cool and dry. Bulbs from this area go dormant in the winter and sprout in response to moisture in the spring. By summer, they are in bloom.

The popularity of bulbs over the centuries has invariably meant that the plants were collected from the wild. This practice has led to the extinction of certain species and near extinction for many others. It is important to buy bulbs from reputable companies that do not collect from the wild—a practice that is illegal in many places. There are more than enough types of bulbs already in cultivation to meet market demands and to further the development of new varieties.

To many people, bulbs in flower—especially lively yellow tulips—mean spring has sprung.

5

FIVE BULB GARDENS

There are many ways to use bulbs in your garden. Choosing a plan that suits your landscape and life-style is the first step in bulb gardening. Here are a few classic examples to stimulate your imagination when planning your garden.

It takes a good understanding of timing and design to execute a flower garden composed entirely of bulbs successfully.

A mixed flower bed combines annuals, perennials and bulbs, and can even include shrubs and small trees.

Outdoor container gardens with bulbs are easy to plant and care for. You can plant annuals right over the bulbs after the bulbs have died back.

Bulbs forced to bloom out of season for indoor placement can be enjoyed like arrangements of cut flowers, but have a longer life.

Naturalized plantings are designed to look as though they occurred on their own. Plant bulbs in an open space where they will multiply for many years.

Types of Bulbs

All bulbs have an enlarged stem or root that increases their capacity for storage. Each type is uniquely adapted to store food for relatively long periods of dormancy so that it can grow and bloom when conditions are optimal.

Rhizomes: Iris and calla

Tuberous roots: Ranunculus and dahlia

True Bulbs: Tulip and lily

8

Tubers: Caladium and tuberous begonia

Corms: Crocus and gladiolus

RECOGNIZING BULBS

The term *bulb* is used to describe five types of storage organs: true bulbs, corms, rhizomes, tubers and tuberous roots. All perform the same basic function of storing food so that the plant can go dormant when conditions are too cold, dry or hot for growth. When conditions improve they sprout, using this reserve for rapid growth and flowering.

A true bulb contains a tiny stem and flower inside many layers of scale-like modified leaves. These leaves, which store food, may be tightly closed and have a protective papery covering, as on a tulip, or they may be more open and lack the papery covering, as on a lily. True bulbs tend to dry out faster than other bulbs, which are solid inside.

A corm is a compact stem with an "eye," or growth bud, at the top that elongates and produces leaves and flowers. Roots grow downward along the base. Other buds on the top or sides produce new corms.

Rhizomes are stems that grow laterally just at or below the soil surface. Buds along the top, at the tip or on the sides produce stems. Roots grow downward along the base.

Tubers are short, thick underground stems. Some are disk-shaped or have disk-shaped areas where the buds grow into stem, leaves and flowers. Roots emerge from the same area as the stems. Tubers increase in size from year to year rather than producing new tubers along the parent.

A tuberous root resembles a tuber; the dahlia and the potato are the best known of the group. Stored food makes up the bulk of the enlarged root. Buds form at one end or at eyes on the surface. Roots grow downward but emerge from all over the main root.

THE BULB LIFE CYCLE

As a bulb begins to sprout, it uses its stored food for energy. At first, the new shoots are too young and growing too fast to make much food on their own. The bulb shrinks as its food reserves are depleted by this rapid burst of growth. As leaves develop they begin to make food for growth, storing any excess in the bulb. The plant proceeds to bud and bloom. Flowering uses up a lot of food energy but the leaves are manufacturing it fast enough to allow the bulb to grow larger and form offsets, which are the beginnings of new plants.

In most true bulbs, these offsets are new bulblets on the sides of the parent. On some true bulbs new growths called bulbils grow out of the stem where the leaves attach.

In corms, the parent dies back completely, but new corms form above the old. They also develop cormels, little corms at the base of the parent.

Rhizomes multiply by growing new sections off the main stem. These sections develop into new plants complete with leaves and flower buds.

Tubers and tuberous roots simply enlarge and develop new eyes.

As the flowers fade on any bulbous plant, seeds are released. (These seeds will develop into bulbs, which may take several years to mature into flowering plants.) The leaves continue to make food and send it to the bulb for storage, but eventually these leaves also fade and dormancy sets in. The bulb and any new offsets it has produced this season now lie dormant, ready to start the cycle again when conditions are favorable.

Dormancy: Every true bulb contains a tiny but fully developed plant, which lies dormant until the right conditions trigger it to grow and bloom.

Growth: Once triggered to grow, the plant uses the food stored in the bulb for energy. Developing leaves begin to make their own food soon after they emerge from the ground.

Flowering: The blooming plant is actually at the end of its life cycle. By now the leaves are manufacturing most of the food for storage and the flower is producing seed.

Dying back: As the flowers fade, the seed ripens. At this point the leaves have finished their job and begin to wilt. The bulb has enlarged with stored food and is ready for dormancy.

Hardy Versus Tender Bulbs

The Cold Factor

Many bulbs that originate in cold-winter climates will not bloom well unless exposed for a certain length of time to temperatures below 45° F. This chilling period triggers root growth that supports flowering in the spring. Without the cold, these plants usually produce a lot of weak growth and few flowers. There are also bulbs that tolerate low temperatures but do not need them in order to bloom well. *Hardy* bulbs, as they are called, grow and bloom almost anywhere. Most spring-blooming bulbs either require cold weather or tolerate it and are usually planted in the fall. This gives their roots, which begin growing almost immediately, plenty of time to develop.

By contrast, many bulbs originating in mild climates will simply die in very cold weather. Often these bulbs bloom in the summer and can be planted in the spring to grow, bloom and then die back by fall. In cold climates, dig them up before the ground freezes and store them in a cool spot protected from freezing. When the weather warms up in spring, plant them again.

Bulbs that bloom in the fall or winter can be hardy or tender depending on the variety. It is best to plant them in the spring so they have plenty of time to develop extensive roots before they bloom. After they bloom, allow hardy bulbs to die back and remain undisturbed until the next blooming season. In cold climates, dig up and store tender fall-blooming bulbs, and do not try to grow tender winter-blooming bulbs outdoors.

Crocus are among the earliest blooming bulbs. Cold does not harm them, and they often emerge right through the snow at the end of winter.

Bulbs Requiring Cold

Crocus
English bluebell
Foxtail lily
Glory-of-the-snow
Lily
Lily-of-the-valley
Narcissus (daffodil)
Puschkinia
Snowdrop
Squill
Tulip (most)
Windflower (some)
Winter aconite

Bulbs Intolerant of Cold

African corn lily
Amaryllis
Baboon flower
Bulbinella
Caladium
Canna
Dahlia
Freesia
Gladiolus
Glory lily
Harlequin flower
Kaffir lily
Nerine
Ranunculus
Spanish bluebell
Spider lily
Tiger flower
Tuberous begonia
Watsonia
Zephyr flower

BULBS FOR ALL SEASONS

Most bulb lovers eventually find themselves striving for year-round bulb color. In many climates this is possible. Even in climates where cool weather rules out late fall and winter flowering outdoors, bulbs can be stimulated, or forced, to bloom indoors.

Plant most summer-blooming bulbs as soon as the soil warms in the spring. Two types of lilies adorn this July garden. The same garden is shown in the small photo above featuring spring color.

Spring-blooming Bulbs Plant spring bloomers such as these daffodils in the fall.

SEASONAL CHOICES

All the plants described in the Bulb Gallery (beginning on page 54) are listed here according to their season of bloom. Keep in mind that these categories are somewhat artificial. Spring in a cold northern climate often arrives as late as May, while in a mild climate it can begin as early as February. Whatever your climate, you can enjoy months of blooming bulbs if you take a little time to plan. Many of the favorite bulbs, especially tulips and narcissus, are sold as early-, mid- or late-season bloomers. Just selecting a variety of bloom times within one type of bulb will lengthen the flowering period in your garden by months.

Be sure to mark where you plant bulbs, so you can plant new bulbs later on without disturbing those already in the ground.

Spring Bloomers
African corn lily, allium, amaryllis, baboon flower, bluebell, brodiaea, calla, camass, cape hyacinth, Chinese ground orchid, crocus, flame freesia, florist's cyclamen, foxtail lily, freesia, fritillary, glory-of-the-snow, grape hyacinth, harlequin flower, hyacinth, iris, kaffir lily, lily-of-the-valley, narcissus, orni-thogalum, oxalis, puschkinia, ranunculus, spring snowflake, spring star flower, squill, tulip, watsonia, windflower, winter aconite

Summer Bloomers
Allium, belladonna lily, blackberry lily, bro-diaea, caladium, canna, dahlia, gladiolus, glory lily, iris, lily, montbretia, summer snowflake, spider lily, tiger flower, tuberous begonia, watsonia, zephyr flower

Fall Bloomers
Canna, florist's cyclamen, lily, meadow saf-fron, nerine, spider lily, sternbergia

Winter Bloomers
Amaryllis, bulbinella, crocus, florist's cycla-men, glory-of-the-snow, kaffir lily, snowdrop, squill, winter aconite

DESIGNING THE GARDEN

The best way to plan a garden, whether incorporating bulbs into a mixed bed or border or planting bulbs alone, is to draw it out on paper. Think it through once you have it roughed out, and apply some of the design basics explained here for a truly pleasing effect.

Planting the Plan
Transfer the scaled dimensions from the plan to the flower bed using chalk or flour for drawing. Identify each section so you'll know where different bulbs are located.

DESIGN BASICS

There are a number of different factors to consider when planning a flower bed. Height, spacing, color, texture and time of flowering are the most important. Taken one at a time, they are quite easy to deal with.

First decide on the size and location of the flower bed. Then study the bed's exposure—how much sun it gets, how windy the spot is and how protected it is from frost and freezing. Remember that in the winter when the sun is low on the horizon it reaches under south-facing eaves but north-facing exposures are shaded. In the summer the sun is directly overhead and reaches more of the north-facing exposure but does not get under eaves or tree canopies facing south.

Once you've chosen the location and considered exposure, you can begin to choose plants and draw them onto your plan. Select plants adapted to your climate and exposure. Remember to consider the time of flowering for each bulb you pick. As you draw your plan, keep tall plants to the back of the bed and short ones to the front. If the bed will be viewed from all sides, put the tall plants in the center and work out to lower plants.

Once you have a rough sketch, you can think about color combinations, leaf texture and shape. It is especially pleasing to mix plants that have upright, sword-shaped leaves with plants that have bushy, rounded leaves. You might also consider other details such as fragrance and cutting potential. Fragrant blooms are best near windows, sitting areas, or the edges of beds or walkways where they can be enjoyed when people pass by. As you add ideas and make adjustments for your tastes and the garden's requirements, you will find that a plan begins to emerge that fills many of your needs.

Begin an all-bulb garden with a small flower bed, seen here midseason and in the photo, at left, just after planting. Expand the bed each year using the same design basics.

17

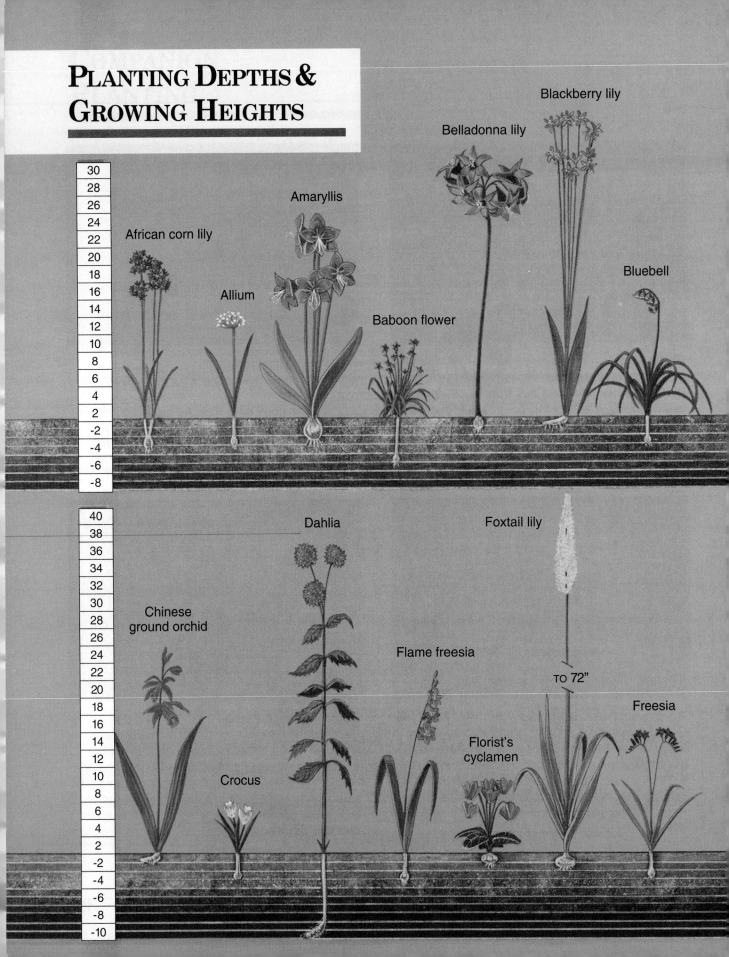

PLANTING DEPTHS & GROWING HEIGHTS

30
28
26
24
22
20
18
16
14
12
10
8
6
4
2
-2
-4
-6
-8

African corn lily

Allium

Amaryllis

Baboon flower

Belladonna lily

Blackberry lily

Bluebell

40
38
36
34
32
30
28
26
24
22
20
18
16
14
12
10
8
6
4
2
-2
-4
-6
-8
-10

Chinese ground orchid

Crocus

Dahlia

Flame freesia

Florist's cyclamen

Foxtail lily

TO 72"

Freesia

Brodiaea

Bulbinella

Caladium

Calla

Camass

Canna

Cape hyacinth

TO 50"

| 46 |
| 44 |
| 42 |
| 40 |
| 38 |
| 36 |
| 34 |
| 32 |
| 30 |
| 28 |
| 26 |
| 24 |
| 22 |
| 20 |
| 18 |
| 16 |
| 14 |
| 12 |
| 10 |
| 8 |
| 6 |
| 4 |
| 2 |
| -2 |
| -4 |
| -6 |
| -8 |

Fritillary

Gladiolus

Glory lily

TO 48"

TO 72"

Glory-of-the-snow

Grape hyacinth

Harlequin flower

Hyacinth

| 40 |
| 38 |
| 36 |
| 34 |
| 32 |
| 30 |
| 28 |
| 26 |
| 24 |
| 22 |
| 20 |
| 18 |
| 16 |
| 14 |
| 12 |
| 10 |
| 8 |
| 6 |
| 4 |
| 2 |
| -2 |
| -4 |
| -6 |
| -8 |
| -10 |

PLANTING DEPTHS & GROWING HEIGHTS

Lily

Iris

Kaffir lily

TO 48"

Montbretia

Lily-of-the-valley

Meadow saffron

| 30 |
| 28 |
| 26 |
| 24 |
| 22 |
| 20 |
| 18 |
| 16 |
| 14 |
| 12 |
| 10 |
| 8 |
| 6 |
| 4 |
| 2 |
| -2 |
| -4 |
| -6 |
| -8 |

Spider lily

Tiger flower

Tuberous begonia

Snowflake

Spring star flower

Squill

Sternbergia

| 40 |
| 38 |
| 36 |
| 34 |
| 32 |
| 30 |
| 28 |
| 26 |
| 24 |
| 22 |
| 20 |
| 18 |
| 16 |
| 14 |
| 12 |
| 10 |
| 8 |
| 6 |
| 4 |
| 2 |
| -2 |
| -4 |
| -6 |
| -8 |

Narcissus

Nerine

Ornithogalum

Oxalis

Puschkinia

Ranunculus

Snowdrop

| 46 |
| 44 |
| 42 |
| 40 |
| 38 |
| 36 |
| 34 |
| 32 |
| 30 |
| 28 |
| 26 |
| 24 |
| 22 |
| 20 |
| 18 |
| 16 |
| 14 |
| 12 |
| 10 |
| 8 |
| 6 |
| 4 |
| 2 |
| -2 |
| -4 |
| -6 |
| -8 |

Watsonia

Tulip

TO 48"

Windflower

Winter aconite

Zephyr flower

| 40 |
| 38 |
| 36 |
| 34 |
| 32 |
| 30 |
| 28 |
| 26 |
| 24 |
| 22 |
| 20 |
| 18 |
| 16 |
| 14 |
| 12 |
| 10 |
| 8 |
| 6 |
| 4 |
| 2 |
| -2 |
| -4 |
| -6 |
| -8 |

CHOOSING BULBS

Bulbs are not all the same. They vary a great deal in size and also in health, or vigor. If you know what to look for when selecting bulbs, your garden will be filled with strong plants and many attractive flowers.

Size Bulbs for any one type of plant come in various grades or sizes. A large, unblemished bulb will produce more flowers and be more likely to survive than a smaller bulb of the same type.

Disease Look for patches of gray or green mold, which signal a weak or diseased bulb. The healthy bulb on the left is dry and firm.

Allowing bulbs to follow their entire cycle of growth, flowering, dying back and dormancy—plus simple garden care—provides year after year of lovely rewards. Here, double early tulips red 'Electra' and white 'Schoonoond' splash across a meadow.

Damage Avoid bulbs with dents, bruises or scars. Their storage tissue is damaged, and this can weaken the plant. The blemish free bulb on the left is a good choice.

What to Look For

When you buy bulbs there are several qualities to look for. Most bulbs are graded according to size. The better the grade, the bigger the bulb, and the more flowers you will probably get from that particular bulb. The prices are higher for the larger bulbs, but the cost is justified by their superior quality. Smaller bulbs may not flower the first year, but they can be a real bargain if you want a lot of bulbs at a good price and if you have the patience to wait a year or two for the best bloom.

Always feel the bulbs before you buy them. Check them over and make sure they are firm. Moldy, bruised or diseased bulbs are fairly easy to detect and are not worth buying. And be sure the displays are well labeled so you can feel confident that you are really getting the color or variety you want.

If you are ordering bulbs from a catalog, use a reputable company. Beware of bargains that seem too good to be true. If you look around and find that the price of the bulbs is far lower than anywhere else, the quality probably is too. Bulb societies and clubs are also a good source for interesting and affordable bulbs.

Once you have the bulbs, plant them as soon as you can. If the weather is still too warm for fall planting—or too cold, if you are planting in the spring—then store the bulbs in paper or net bags. Plastic bags are airtight, and the bulbs will rot in them. Place the bulbs in a dark spot that is cool but protected from freezing. The goal of storage is to keep the bulbs from sprouting and using up their stored energy before the roots have a chance to grow.

Rot If the bulb feels soft or mushy, some type of rot has ruined the interior. The bulb on the left is firm and doesn't dent when gently pressed.

Dessication Fleshy bulbs may have dry outer leaves. These bulbs should be fat and firm. Do not buy any bulbs if they are withered or dried out.

PREPARING TO PLANT

GOOD SOIL

The most important step to a successful garden is to begin with good soil. The soil in most new garden beds needs some work before it is in shape for planting. First figure out what type of soil you have. To determine your soil's pH (acidity or alkalinity), you can buy a kit at the nursery and test it. Or check to see if your county Agricultural Extension office provides this service. There are also private companies that will test your soil for a fee. These tests tend to be more accurate than those done with do-it-yourself kits, and they give you more information.

You also need to know if your soil is mostly clay or sand. If your soil is sandy, water drains through it very quickly and the soil falls apart when you squeeze a handful and then open up your hand. Conversely, water soaks into clay soil slowly and if you squeeze a handful, it will hold its shape when you open your hand. Ideal soil holds its shape when you squeeze it but falls apart easily if you tap it with a finger.

All three types of soil benefit from the addition of organic matter. It loosens up clay soil, helps retain moisture and hold together sandy soil, and further enhances the structure of good soil. You can start a compost pile and make your own organic soil amendment or buy bags of ready-to-use compost.

If your soil is very acidic or alkaline, use compost to help buffer either condition. Acidic soils also benefit from applications of lime. This amendment, purchased at garden centers, lowers the acidity of soil. Alkaline soils can benefit temporarily from the addition of gypsum. Deep watering also helps by leaching out the salts that increase alkalinity.

Double-Digging

First Double-digging is a method of preparing the soil so roots grow strong and deep. Start by outlining the bulb bed with garden lime or flour.

Then Clear out any weeds or debris in the area to be planted. Cut and roll sod for disposal if the bed is in an existing lawn area.

Third Remove 8–10 in. of soil off to the side of the bed. This can be done by rows, digging one row at a time if the bed is large, or one planting hole at a time for scattered installations.

Fourth Use a garden fork to loosen the subsoil another 8–10 in. Remove any large stones you unearth.

Next Add 4–6 in. of organic amendment to the subsoil and mix it in. This provides nutrients for roots that reach this level.

Last Return the topsoil mixed with some super-phosphate and fertilizer. Rake and level the bed; water it well and allow the soil to settle for a day before planting.

Superphosphate is a fertilizer that helps the bulb roots grow well. Add it to the planting hole before placing the bulb.

PLANTING BULBS

Once the planning and designing is done and the soil is prepared, you can plant the bulbs. Use the guide on pages 20–23 for information on planting depths and bulb orientation.

Most bulbs look very effective planted in odd-numbered groups. Planting bulbs makes a good family project.

SUPERPHOSP
0-25-0

How to Plant a Bulb

First Once the soil is prepared, dig a 6–12 in. hole, depending upon the type of bulb.

Then Sprinkle superphosphate into the bottom of the hole if you have not added it to the bed yet. Follow label directions.

Third Place the bulb in the hole—pointed end up and knob side down. Space bulbs 4–6 in. apart, depending upon the type of bulb.

Last Cover the bulb with soil, tamping firmly. Water the area thoroughly. After the leaves appear, it is not necessary to water again unless the weather is dry.

Year-round Bulb Care

Throughout the year there are a few tasks that help maintain the appearance of the flower bed and keep bulbs growing vigorously.

Marking After planting new bulbs, mark their location so that you can plant around them without inadvertently digging one up, cutting into one or planting on top of one.

Weeding Weeds compete for water and nutrients in the soil. Do your best to keep the beds weed free so the new bulbs have the best possible conditions for strong growth.

You certainly can't tell a flower from its bulb. This Darwin tulip, 'Dutch Fair,' with a bright yellow bloom stripped with orange, came from a simple brown true bulb.

Mulching A layer of mulch around plants, or over the entire bed before sprouts show, holds in moisture and inhibits weeds. Weeds that do grow up through mulch are easier to remove.

Watering Dampen the soil before installing bulbs and water well after covering the bulbs with soil. Regular watering that keeps the soil consistently moist but not soggy will encourage rapid, vigorous growth.

Staking Tall plants that tend to flop over should be staked, especially if you are in a windy area. Plants that flop to the ground get less sun and are exposed to pests and soil-borne diseases.

Fertilizing A regular application of fertilizer once the plants have sprouted increases the size and vigor of the plants and flowers. It will also help increase flower production the following year. Follow label instructions.

Deadheading When flowers fade, cut them off so the plant does not waste energy trying to make seeds. Their energy is best used to increase the bulb size.

CONTROLLING PESTS & DISEASES

Good health is the best weapon against pests and diseases. Light infestations do relatively little damage to a well-maintained plant. When the problem is severe, eradication methods may be necessary to save the bulb. Always follow label instructions when using pesticides and fungicides.

Aphids Leaves curl and distort and sometimes yellow. Often, there is a shiny, sticky substance on the leaves. You may see tiny yellow, green or dark insects. Wash them off with sharp spray from the hose. If the infestation is severe, spray with insecticide containing diazinon or malathion.

Bulb maggots (narcissus bulb fly larvae) Bulbs are soft when squeezed. They do not produce flowers, and small bumblebee-like insects appear in the spring. Buy only healthy bulbs. As a precaution, dust bulbs with trichlorfon dust before planting.

Bulb rots (fungus or bacterial disease) Bulbs are mushy and have stunted, wilting, yellowing leaves. Buy only healthy bulbs and plant them in well-drained soil. As a precaution, dip new bulbs in a solution of truban before planting. Dig up and discard infected bulbs.

Botrytis Brown spots appear that are covered with gray fuzz. Often called gray mold, botrytis affects flowers and foliage. It is difficult to control and spreads quickly. Dig up and discard diseased bulbs.

Mites Leaves have tiny spots on their surfaces and webbing on their backs. Plants grow well until heavily infested. Chemical sprays are available, but a sharp spray from the hose usually washes away mites.

Borers Eggs hatch in the leaves of irises, and the pest bores through the plant to the bulb. Streaks in the leaves appear in spring. Keep the planted area clean of debris. Dust regularly with carbaryl, dimethoate or malathion in the spring.

Leaf spots Very small brown, gray, yellow or red spots appear and spread. Leaves may turn yellow and die. Many types of fungus cause leaf spots. Warm, damp weather encourages the problem. Discard infected leaves. Spray with copper sulfate.

Rodents Bulbs do not grow. When dug up they look chewed. Surround bulbs with chicken wire when planting to prevent gopher and squirrel damage. If mice are the problem, cover the bed with hardware cloth; remove it as shoots emerge.

Thrips Silvery streaks show up on leaves, and the tips die back. Tiny, $\frac{1}{20}$ in. long insects can sometimes be seen. Pick off infested leaves or spray the plant with acephate or carbaryl insecticides.

Powdery mildew The upper surfaces of leaves show white or gray powdery patches. Leaves yellow and die. This fungus spreads rapidly. Spray with a fungicide containing triforine. Clean up and discard diseased leaves and debris.

Slugs and snails Holes in the leaves and silvery trails on the leaves and on the ground around plants indicate the presence of these pests. Look for pests feeding at night. Remove them by hand or spread bait around the base of affected plants.

Viruses Leaves are yellow and may be streaked or mottled. Flowers may be streaked or blotched. There is no cure, but mild infections are not harmful. Remove severely infected plants and any infected lilies. Clean tools and hands after touching plants to avoid spreading the virus.

END-OF-SEASON CARE

WINDING DOWN THE GROWING SEASON

As bulb flowers fade, many gardeners are tempted to cut off the foliage in order to tidy up the garden. But the best thing you can do for your bulb plants is to continue to nurture them until they are truly finished growing for the season. The longer the leaves stay green and healthy, the longer the plant is producing and storing food for next year's growth. More food storage means more numerous and larger flowers next year.

Water and feed foliage as long as it looks good. As the leaves begin to fade and droop, water less often and discontinue feeding. Most bulbs do best if the leaves are allowed to die back completely before being removed. Then the dried, dead foliage simply pulls away. If it does not come away easily, wait a few days before trying again.

Avoid braiding or knotting spent-looking foliage; it will be less able to photosynthesize and produce food for storage. If the dying foliage really bothers you, plant some tall or bushy annuals in front of the bulbs to hide them as they die back. You can also plant a garden with perennials that will cover the foliage of spring bulbs. Many of the perennial daisies (*Chrysanthemum* species) and asters perform this function well. As the perennial plants begin to grow in the spring, they are too small to interfere with your view of the blooming bulbs. But by the time the bulbs begin to fade, the perennials have grown up enough to hide them.

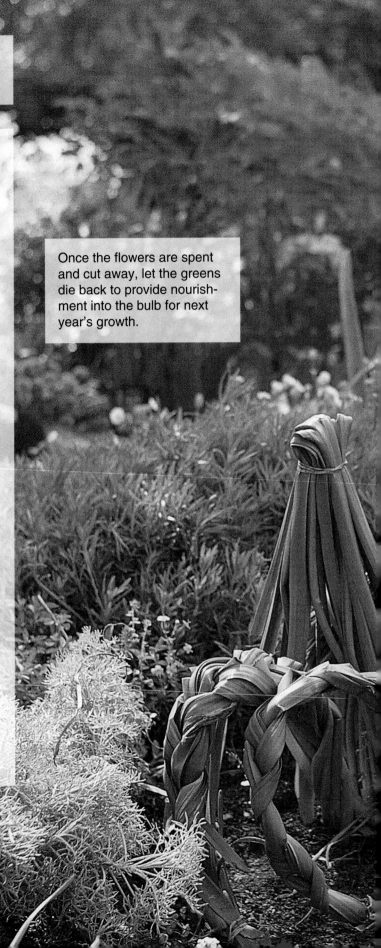

Once the flowers are spent and cut away, let the greens die back to provide nourishment into the bulb for next year's growth.

Storing Tender Bulbs

First Using a garden fork, dig and lift tender bulbs from the garden before cold weather sets in. Gently shake off the soil.

Next Dust the bulbs with fungicide powder to prevent rot. Store them in a paper bag, net or old hosiery—something that allows ventilation. Do not use plastic.

Last Hang bulbs in a cool, dark, dry spot that is protected from freezing.

DIVIDING BULBS

Often after several years bulb plantings begin to look crowded and do not bloom as well as they once did. You can divide your mature bulbs to encourage vigorous growth and to increase the number of bulbs you have.

After several years, dig up and divide bulbs such as these Dutch iris. These bulbs, propagated in your garden, make great gifts.

Dividing Rhizomes and Tuberous Roots

First With a garden fork, carefully dig and lift overcrowded bearded iris rhizomes after they have stopped blooming.

Next Use a clean knife to cut them apart at narrow sections of the rhizome. Each new piece should have at least one fan of leaves.

Last Trim the leaves to 4 in. and plant the new sections just deep enough to cover the rhizome. Water thoroughly.

Dividing Other Bulbs

True Bulbs New bulbs grow to the side of the parent. Dig and lift the parent bulbs and gently break off the new ones. Replant both the original and the offspring.

Corms As the original corm dies, a new one develops above it. Little cormels may also be present along the base of the new corm. These bloom in about 2 years.

Tubers Tubers enlarge over time and can be cut up to produce several plants. Each new piece must contain at least one growing point.

LETTING BULBS NATURALIZE

THE NATURALIZED GARDEN

"Naturalized" bulbs are bulbs that grow and multiply in an open area with a minimum of care. They must be a type that is suited to your climate; that is, adapted to the minimum and maximum temperatures and the annual rainfall for your location. They are most often planted in a wild area—one that is not obviously or formally landscaped. Here they can follow their annual cycle, growing without intervention for years.

Once planted, this type of garden requires very little maintenance. An occasional feeding will speed the proliferation of the bulbs and enhance flowering, but it is not necessary. The only real work occurs when the bulbs have spread so completely that they need thinning. Even then, they will crowd themselves and naturally thin out on their own, although this process may create unwanted gaps. If you want to, dig and divide the crowded areas and replant the bulbs according to your own design.

There are only a few rules for creating a naturalized bulb landscape. First, plant in a natural pattern—which means no pattern at all. Straight lines or evenly spaced clumps do not look created by nature. A tried-and-true method is to toss the bulbs around the allotted area and plant them where they fall. This not only produces a perfectly unstructured pattern, it also ensures open, loose spacing, which allows the bulbs to multiply for many years without getting crowded. It is a good idea to place some superphosphate in the hole as you plant each bulb, just as you would in a more traditional bulb garden. And if rainfall is below average, water the area.

Naturalizing Bulbs

Allium
Belladonna lily
Brodiaea
Camass
Crocus
Fritillary
Glory-of-the-snow
Grape hyacinth
Iris reticulata
Meadow saffron
Narcissus
Ornithogalum
Snowflake
Squill
Tulip (some)
Winter aconite

Bulbs look as though they are growing wild when planted in drifts in an informal part of the yard.

BULBS FOR SHADY PLACES

THE SHADE GARDEN

There are a few important cultural needs in a shade garden. Shaded areas are often confined or slightly enclosed, and moisture can build up, encouraging potentially harmful fungus or disease. Adequate air circulation improves these conditions, so it's best to space plants farther apart than you would otherwise, especially if the air is very still. Shaded gardens do not dry out as fast and therefore need less water than sites in full sun. Check the soil moisture often when your shade garden is new so you can learn to apply the optimum amount of water.

Gardeners identify different degrees of shade. Deep shade is the heaviest shade. You will find deep shade between tall buildings or under the canopy of large trees.

Medium shade can be found on the north sides of buildings where it is open and bright but there is little or no direct sun. It can also be found under the canopy of trees with an open branch pattern. Only a few type of bulbs grow in this light.

Light shade is also called partial shade. It is found in bright locations that are protected from full sun by foliage or in areas that get full sun for the first part of the day only. An area that gets full sun in the afternoon is usually too hot to support a plant that needs any degree of shade.

Remember that the degree of shade a location receives may vary as trees and shrubs go through the seasons.

Recommendations for exposure refer to the amount of sun a bulb will receive when it is growing and flowering.

Combine shade loving caladiums and tuberous begonia in containers and place them where they can be best enjoyed, such as near a shady seat.

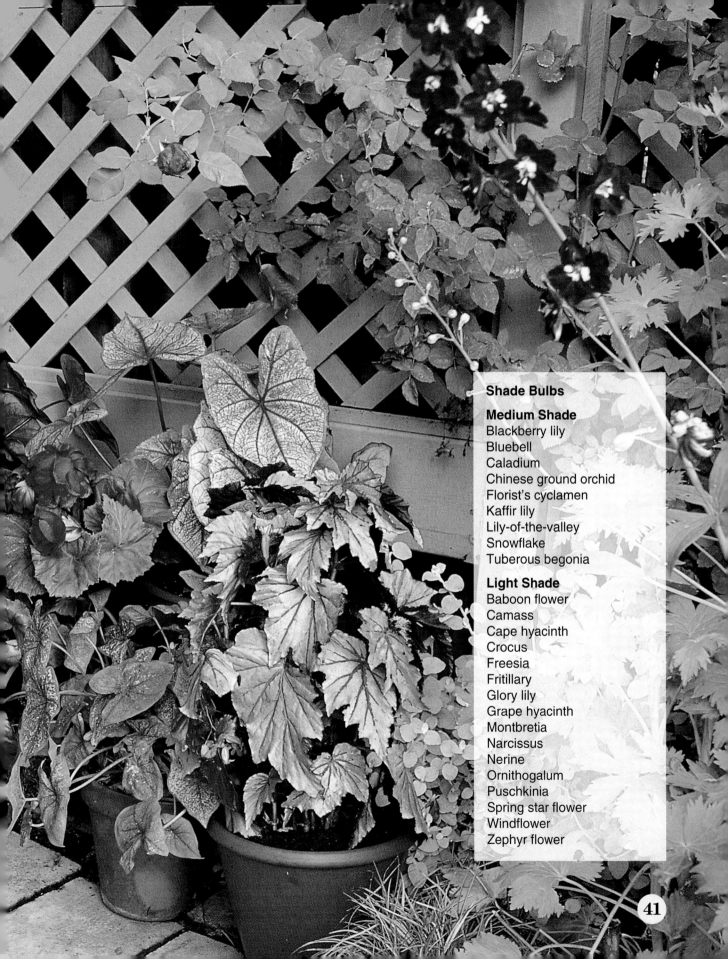

Shade Bulbs

Medium Shade
Blackberry lily
Bluebell
Caladium
Chinese ground orchid
Florist's cyclamen
Kaffir lily
Lily-of-the-valley
Snowflake
Tuberous begonia

Light Shade
Baboon flower
Camass
Cape hyacinth
Crocus
Freesia
Fritillary
Glory lily
Grape hyacinth
Montbretia
Narcissus
Nerine
Ornithogalum
Puschkinia
Spring star flower
Windflower
Zephyr flower

BULBS FOR FRAGRANCE

Besides beauty, some bulbs have the added attraction of fragrance. These plants are especially desirable, and none more so than the sweet-smelling, spring-blooming bulbs that in one breath sweep away the dull pall of winter.

Fragrant Bulbs

Allium
Belladonna lily
Cape hyacinth
Crocus (some)
Freesia
Grape hyacinth
Hyacinth
Iris
Lily
Lily-of-the-valley
Narcissus (some)
Winter aconite

THE SCENTED GARDEN

Most gardeners choose fragrant bulbs for both their visual appeal and their perfume. But planting bulbs for their fragrance is a wasted effort if you cannot get close to the blossoms. For full enjoyment bring the plants indoors in pots or grow them along a walkway, under a window or near a bench.

For the most part, all would agree that fragrant flowers complement gardens and floral displays. But what smells good to one person may not to another. Most of the commonly grown bulbs that are fragrant have a very strong perfume. And generally these bulbs are chosen partly for this quality. But there are many people who find the heavy, sweet scent of hyacinth just a bit overwhelming. And paper-white narcissus, a favorite for forced indoor blooming, also seems too strong to many people. These are beautiful flowers and deserve a place in the garden—just a bit farther back if you do not appreciate their strong scent.

It is also interesting to note that although most people are able to enjoy the fragrance of freesias, there is a small percentage of the population who just cannot smell their perfume. For those few, planting freesias for their beauty alone can still be worthwhile.

Some people think that certain flowers smell better "back home," attributing this to the climate or better growing conditions. The truth is, a particular flower will smell the same no matter where it is grown; however, many plants have been bred for qualities such as color or flower size, and in the process their scent has been lost. It's important to read bulb descriptions carefully to be sure you are getting a variety that produces the flower and scent you want.

Position fragrant freesia near paths and patios where you can enjoy their visual and olfactory delights.

BULBS FOR CUTTING

HOW TO CUT FLOWERS

You can extend the vase life of cut flowers by many days if you take good care of them from the start. There are several important rules to follow. The first is to cut the flowers early or late in the day but never when they are in full sun on a warm day; if it is overcast, cut them anytime. This timing ensures that the flowers are as full of water as possible. Plants lose water rapidly in the hot sun and will dry out very quickly if cut.

The next step is to immediately plunge the cut stems into a bucket of water that you have brought with you into the garden. Then take the flowers indoors and place them in a sink filled with warm water. Cut the stems again under water. This second cut is important. Plants move water up their stems through tension. When you cut the stem, a small air pocket is sucked into the stem and slowly moves up. The air pocket prevents water from moving up the stem and can bring on early wilting or cause the "neck" of the flower to bend. By immediately cutting about a half-inch off the stem under water, you cut off this bubble and avoid introducing another one. Now you can feel free to move the stems in and out of the water while you arrange them. Just try not to keep the flowers out of water for an extended period.

Many commercially available water treatments will also help preserve cut flowers. They usually come in powdered form and contain sugar to feed the plants and disinfectant to inhibit bacterial growth, which clogs the stems. These powders are mixed into the water and work well. You can make your own solution by adding about ten drops of chlorine bleach and a tablespoon of sugar to a gallon of water.

Gladiolus make stunning cut flowers in indoor arrangements. Plant part of your garden specifically for cutting; the savings between buying bulbs and buying florist flowers is considerable.

Cutting Bulbs

Allium
Dahlia
Freesia
Fritillary
Gladiolus
Hyacinth
Iris
Lily
Lily-of-the-valley
Montbretia
Narcissus
Nerine
Ornithogalum
Peruvian daffodil
Ranunculus
Snowflake
Spring star flower
Sternbergia
Tulip
Watsonia

Cut Flower Care

First Cut the blooms, leaving some foliage behind to provide food for the bulb. Recut the stems under warm water, removing ½ in. from the ends.

Next Select a vase and mix a flower preservative into the water. Arrange the flowers. Be especially careful with flowers that have a hollow stem; they bend and damage easily.

Last Recut the stems after about 5 days. If you did not add a preservative to the water, trim the stems and replace the water every day to extend the vase life of the flowers.

THE INDOOR GARDEN

There are two categories of bulbs to grow in your home. The first includes bulbs that you can simply plant in a pot, place in a bright spot, keep watered and watch bloom. Bringing them into the house may hasten blooming, especially in winter. All they need to trigger growth is the warmth of indoors. The second category includes bulbs that require a period of cold before they will bloom. These are discussed on pages 50–51.

For indoor bloom, probably the easiest and most common bulb is fragrant paperwhite narcissus. You can pot it in soil, stones or marbles, or even just set it half submerged in a vase of water. It will grow roots, send up leaves and bloom in four to six weeks. Paper-white narcissus is popular because it has a strong, sweet fragrance that has become a popular Christmas decoration for many people. The smell and sight of these spring-blooming plants in December is quite cheering.

Another very popular and easy bulb is the amaryllis. This huge bulb puts up a thick stem with blossoms up to eight inches across. Plant it in a container that is just a few inches larger around than the bulb, with the narrow neck of the bulb above the soil surface. Keep the soil evenly moist, and place the container in bright but indirect light. Amaryllis is one of the few bulbs that will bloom year after year indoors. After all the flowers have faded, cut off the stem at the base. If leaves are not already growing, they will begin to grow now. Keep the plant fed and watered until the leaves yellow, then cut them off and store the potted bulb in a cool, dark place protected from freezing. Do not water it. The following winter, bring the plant back into a bright, warm room and keep it watered. The amaryllis will bloom again.

Indoor Bulbs

Amaryllis
Caladium
Florist's cyclamen
Freesia
Glory lily
Kaffir lily
Narcissus (some)
Nerine
Ornithogalum
Tuberous begonia
Zephyr flower

Amaryllis and paper white narcissus both grow well indoors, have fabulous scents and bloom in winter, making them ideal nontraditional holiday decorations.

OUT-OF-SEASON BLOOMING

Bulbs that require a period of cold before they will flower can be stimulated to bloom by placing them in the refrigerator or outdoors for a short "winter" and then bringing them inside where it is warm for an early "spring." This process is called *forcing*.

Forced Bulbs

Brodiaea
Crocus
Dutch iris
Grape hyacinth
Hyacinth
Iris reticulata
Narcissus
Ornithogalum
Snowdrop
Squill
Tulip
Winter aconite

Combining many flowering bulbs in a container and bringing it indoors for winter color can go a long way towards chasing the clouds away. Here, tulips and hyacinth require chilling to bloom early. Narcissus, freesia and glory-of-the-snow will bloom without the need of forcing.

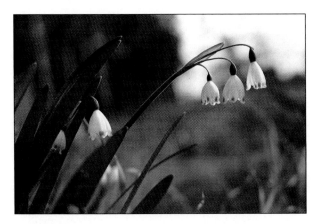

Snowflake
Leucojum species
L. vernum, the 6–10 in. spring snowflake, and the slightly larger *L. aestivum,* the summer snowflake, have white bell flowers with green marks on each petal. They are hardy in Zones 4 to 10. *L. autumnale,* grown in Zones 4 to 10, is just 6 in. and bears pinkish blooms soon after planting in fall. Plant the bulbs 3 in. deep in light to medium shade. These plants require well-drained soil and regular watering.

Spring star flower
Ipheion uniflorum
Spring star flowers grow 6–8 in. The grassy leaves are blue-green and the same height as the blossom. Plant bulbs 2 in. deep in the fall in full sun to light shade. They are hardy to Zone 6. Flower color, depending on the cultivar, ranges from white with a bit of blue to deep blue. They do well in any soil and require regular watering while growing.

Spider lily
Lycoris species
The spider lily is closely related to the belladonna lily. Foliage dies back before the 2-ft. stems grow out to produce large white, yellow, pink or red blooms in late summer to fall. Plant bulbs just below the soil surface in late summer in a sunny spot. Hardiness varies with the species. In cold climates, plant the bulbs in containers. These plants require well-drained soil and regular watering when they are in a growing phase.

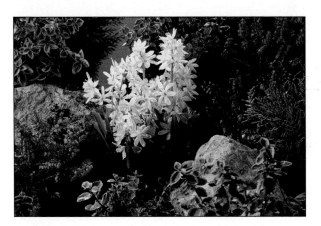

Squill
Scilla species
Flowers are white, pink, violet or blue and grow 6–12 in. Plant these bulbs 2–4 in. deep in autumn for winter to spring bloom. Squill prefers sun while flowering and light shade in summer. Species vary in hardiness: *S. peruviana* grows to just Zone 9, while *S. bifolia* grows down to Zone 3. These plants require rich, well-drained soil, and regular watering while growing.

BULB GALLERY
Tulipa species and hybrids

Tulips are a sure sign that spring has arrived. The flowers can be white, cream, yellow, orange, maroon, purple, lavender, red, pink or multi-colored. These tough bulbs are hardy down to Zone 3 and most need cold winters to bloom year after year. In Zones 9 and 10 they seldom bloom a second year; treat them like annuals. Plant 4–6 inches deep in the fall in sun or very light shade.

Mid-season tulips
This second wave of bloomers includes several hybrids. Darwin hybrid tulips such as 'Ivory Floradale,' top above, bloom earlier than their parent. The 30-in. stems hold very large blooms in vivid reds and oranges. 'Big Chief' is rosy salmon and 'General Eisenhower' is bright red. Mendel tulips, also derived from hybrids and crosses with Darwin tulips, are single and bloom in white, yellow, orange, pink or red on 20-in. stems. Triumph tulips have thicker stems, up to 20 in. long with white, yellow, red or bicolor blooms. 'Apricot Beauty,' above, is a salmon and apricot blend.

Early season tulips
These are the first tulips to appear in spring. The single types grow on 10–15 in. stems with large blossoms. They are the best types to force in pots for winter indoor color. The double flowers grow on 6–12 in. stems and reach up to 4 in. across. These can also be forced indoors. There are many cultivars to choose from, including salmon-and-orange-striped 'Princess Irene,' top above, and the fringed tulip 'Blue Heron,' above.

Late-season tulips

Darwin tulips are probably the most popular of the late-season tulips, with 20–30 in. stems and large oval blooms with square bases. Colors include white, yellow, orange, pink, lilac, purple or red. Lily-flowered tulips have narrow, pointed petals with a lily-like appearance. The long petals curve back and bloom in white, yellow, pink or red. Cottage tulips, with flowers in white, yellow, orange, pink, purple or red, resemble Darwins in size, height and oval shape. Rembrandt tulips are streaked or variegated with different colors. They are called "broken" tulips because of their coloration. Parrot tulips, top above, bloom in May and are also broken with striped or feathered petals. The petals are large and long with fringed or ruffled edges. Multistemmed tulips such as 'Orange Sorbet,' above, grow to 24 in. and bloom in white, yellow, orange or rose. There are many cultivars of each type to choose from.

Species tulips

These are good choices for mild-winter areas that do not provide the winter chilling required by most tulips. *T. fosteriana* is an early-season plant with red 4–8 in. blooms on 8–20 in. stems 'Red Emperor' is the most widely recognized cultivar. *T. kaufmanniana,* top above, is an early-season tulip with 4–8 in. stems and open, flat, pointed petals in cream to yellow with bright yellow centers and red markings on the outside. *T. turkestanica,* above, with its multi flowered stems, makes a spectacular spot planting.

Bulb Gallery

Tiger flower, Mexican shell flower
Tigridia pavonia
This true bulb blooms in summer and has lance-shaped, pleated leaves up to 18 in. long. The 3-petaled flowers grow up to 6 in. across, and each 12–30 in. stem carries many blooms in purple, red, orange, pink, yellow or white. Plant in full sun to light shade 2–4 in. deep in spring. Tiger flower is hardy to Zone 7; elsewhere dig and store bulbs over winter. It requires well-drained soil and regular watering while growing.

Tuberous begonia
Begonia x *tuberhybrida*
Tremendous variety in both flower color and shape characterizes these showy summer-blooming 12–18 in. plants. Colors range from red, orange, yellow, pink, and cream to white. Place tubers just below the soil surface in light to medium shade in spring when frost is past. Begonias must be dug and stored over winter except in Zone 10. They require rich, moist soil.

Sternbergia
Sternbergia lutea
Bright yellow, crocus-like blooms appear atop 5–9 in. stems in early fall. Foliage grows through winter and dies back in spring. Plant bulbs 4 in. deep in mid to late summer. Sternbergia is hardy to Zone 6 if given winter protection. It needs full sun and well-drained soil. Water regularly while the plant is growing.

Watsonia, bugle lily
Watsonia species
These spring and summer bloomers grow up to 6 ft.
with double rows of white, apricot, red, salmon, pink or
lavender flowers. Plant corms 4 in. deep in full sun in
fall in mild climates. These plants are hardy to Zone 8.
In Zones 7 and colder, plant in the spring; dig and store
the bulbs over winter. They grow in any soil and need
regular watering while growing.

Winter aconite
Eranthis hyemalis
Sweet-smelling, cup-shaped, butter yellow flowers grow
to 8 in. in late winter to early spring. Hardy to Zone 4,
winter aconite needs cold to do well. Plant tubers 3 in.
deep in fall in a spot with winter and spring sun but a bit
of summer shade, preferably under deciduous trees or
shrubs. It needs rich, moist, well-drained soil.

Windflower
Anemone blanda, A. coronaria
Plant tubers in fall or spring in full sun to light shade for
spring bloom. *A. blanda* is a white, pink, rose or blue
daisy-like flower on an 8-in. stem that thrives to Zone 6.
A. coronaria, shown here, the poppy anemone, with
larger, poppy-like flowers blooms in blue, white, red or
pink, grows to 18 in. and thrives to Zone 7. It needs rich,
well-drained soil. Keep soil dry through the summer.

Zephyr flower, fairy lily
Zephyranthes species
Late-summer blossoms of white, yellow or pink grow to
12 in. above grassy foliage. Plant bulbs 1–2 in. deep in
early fall in full sun to light shade. Plants may bloom
more than once in mild climates if allowed to dry out and
then watered again regularly. In Zones 8 and colder,
plant in the spring and dig and store bulbs over winter.
Zephyr flower needs well-drained soil and regular water.

PLANTING ZONE MAP

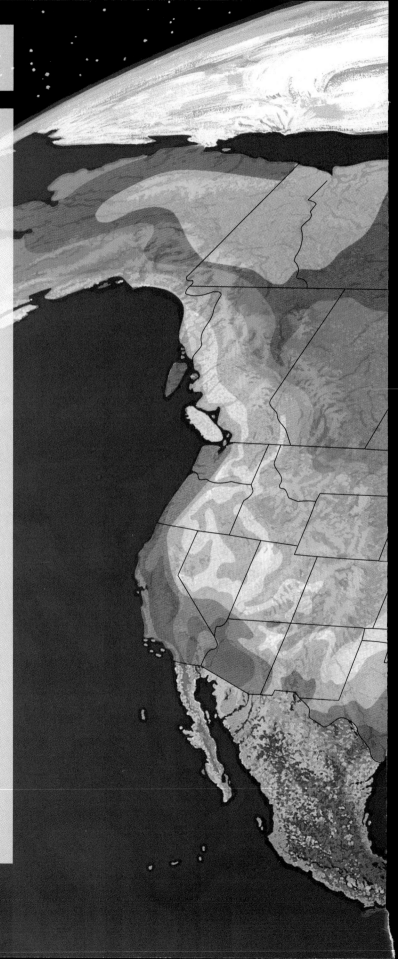

HOW TO USE THIS MAP

The map outlines eleven zones in North America for the purpose of determining plant hardiness. It is based on the United States Department of Agriculture's figures for minimum winter temperatures.

It's important to understand that the zones are designed to provide basic information, not absolute parameters.

You may, for example, live very near a zone border or in a microclimate such as a sunny, south-facing valley. If that's the case, you may have slightly higher temperatures more like those in the next warmer zone. Or perhaps you're near the highest elevation of your region in a windy spot with temperatures more like the next cooler zone.

Good winter protection will extend the life of your bulbs in marginal zones where plants may be in danger during the coldest months. Use a protective layer of mulch—such as leaves, evergreen boughs or straw—over the plants. The colder it is or the less hardy the plant, the more mulch you need. Use a foot or more if you're in Zone 3 or cooler or are in the coldest recommended zone for a particular plant. Fall mulching helps keep crowns from freezing and thawing repeatedly.

On the other hand, you may live where heat is the source of potential damage to your bulbs. Shade from arbors or trees will help keep afternoon sun from damaging plants. Regular watering and a moisture-saving layer of mulch on the soil also help.

Watching and working with nature is part of the excitement and challenge gardening offers. Whether it's adapting to nature's sometimes harsh conditions or reveling in the beauty of a single flower, true satisfaction comes from the ongoing process of making the garden the best it can be.

ZONE 1
Winters below −50°F.

ZONE 2
Winters −50° to −40° F.

ZONE 3
Winters −40° to −30° F.

ZONE 4
Winters −30° to −20° F.

ZONE 5
Winters −20° to −10° F.

ZONE 6
Winters −10° to 0° F.

ZONE 7
Winters 0° to 10° F.

ZONE 8
Winters 10° to 20° F.

ZONE 9
Winters 20° to 30° F.

ZONE 10
Winters 30° to 40° F.

ZONE 11
Winters above 40° F.

INDEX

A

African corn lily (*Lxia maculata*), 54
allium (*Allium* species), 54
Amaryllis belladonna, 55
amaryllis (*Hippeastrum* Dutch hybrids), 54
Anemone blanda, 75
Anemone coronaria, 75
annual cover, 19
annual flowers, 18
aphids, 32
Apricot Beauty tulips, 72
Asiatic hybrids, 64
Aurelian hybrids, 64
autumn crocus (*Colchicum* species), 66

B

baboon flower (*Babiana* species), 55
Begonia x tuberhybrida, 74
Belamcanda chinensis, 55
belladonna lily, naked lady (*Amaryllis belladonna*), 55
Big Chief tulips, 72
blackberry lily (*Belamcanda chinensis*), 55
Bletilla striata, 58
bluebell (*Endymion* species), 55
Blue Heron tulips, 72
borers, 32
botrytis, 32
brodiaea (*Brodiaea, Dichelostemma* and *Triteleia* species), 56
bugle lily (*Watsonia* species), 75
bulb data chart, 52-53
bulb gardens

companion planting in, 18-19
container, 46-47
designing, 16-17
five examples of, 6-7
indoor, 49
naturalized, 38-39
scented, 42-43
shady, 40-41
bulb life cycle, 10-11
bulb maggots, 32
bulb rots, 32
bulbs
benefits of growing, 4
choosing, 24-25
for cutting, 44-45
depths/growing heights of, 20-23
dividing, 36
end-of-season care for, 34-35
for fragrance, 42-43
historical origins of, 5
indoor, 49
for outdoor containers, 46-47
out-of-season blooming, 50-51
planting, 28-29
seasonal, 14-15
for shady places, 40-41
tender vs. hardy, 12-13
types of, 8-9
year-round care of, 30-31

C

caladium (*Caladium* x *hortulanum*), 56
calla (*Zantadeschia aethiopica*), 57
camass (*Camassia* species), 57
candidum hybrids, 65
canna (*Canna* hybrids), 57

Cape hyacinth (*Galtonia candicans*), 57
Chinese ground orchid (*Bletilla striata*), 58
Chionodoxa species, 61
Colchicum species, 66
cold factor, 12-13
companion planting, 18-19
container bulbs, 46-47
Convallaria majalis, 66
corms
described, 9
dividing, 37
crested iris (*Iris cristata*), 62
Crocosmia x *crocosmiiflora,* 67
crocus (*Crocus* species), 58
cutting bulbs, 44-45
Cyclamen persicum, 59
cyclamineus hybrids, 68

D

daffodils, 68-69
dahlia (*Dahlia* hybrids), 58
damaged bulbs, 24
deadheading, 31
dessication (bulbs), 25
Dichelostemma species, 56
diseases
controlling, 32-33
identifying bulbs with, 24
dormancy, 10
double-digging, 27
double narcissi, 68
Dutch iris, 62
dying back, 11

E

early season tulips, 72
Endymion species, 55
Eranthis hyemalis, 75
Eremurus species, 59

F

fairy lily (*Zephyranthes* species), 75
fall-blooming bulbs, 15
fertilizing, 27, 31
flame freesia (*Tritonia* species), 59
florist's cyclamen (*Cyclamen persicum*), 59
flowering period, 11
forced bulbs, 50-51
foxtail lily (*Eremurus* species), 59
freesia (*Freesia* hybrids), 59
fritillary (*Fritillaria* species), 60

G

Galanthus species, 70
Galtonia candicans, 57
General Eisenhower tulips, 72
gladiolus (*Gladiolus* x *hortulanus*), 60
glory lily (*Gloriosa rothschildiana*), 60
glory-of-the-snow (*Chionodoxa* species), 61
grape hyacinth (*Muscari* species), 61
ground cover, 19
growing heights, 20-23
growth period, 10

H

hardy bulbs, 12-13
harlequin flower (*Sparaxis tricolor*), 61
Hippeastrum Dutch hybrids, 54
hyacinth (*Hyacinthus orientalis*), 61

I

indoor bulbs, 49
Ipheion uniflorum, 71
Iris cristata, 62
Iris species, 62-63
Ivory Floradale tulips, 72

J

Japanese iris, 63
Jonquilla hybrids, 68

K

kaffir lily, 66

L

large-cupped narcissi, 68
late-season tulips, 73
leaf spots, 33
Leucojum species, 71
Lilium species, 64-65
Lily-of-the-valley (*Convallaria majalis*), 66
longiflorum hybrids, 65
Lxia maculata, 54
Lycoris species, 71

M

marking bulb location, 30
meadow saffron, autumn crocus (*Colchicum* species), 66
Mexican shell flower (*Tigridia pavonia*), 74
mid-season tulips, 72
mites, 32
montbretia (*Crocosmia* x *crocosmiiflora*), 67
mulching, 30
Muscari species, 61

N

naked lady (*Amaryllis belladonna*), 55
Narcissus species, 68-69
naturalizing bulbs, 38-39
nerine (*Nerine* species), 67

O

Orange Sorbet tulips, 72
Oriental hybrids, 65
ornithogalum (*Ornithogalum* species), 67
out-of-season blooming, 50-51
oxalis (*Oxalis tetraphylla*), 67

P

perennials, 19
pest control, 32-33
planting
   bulbs, 28-29
   in container, 46-47
planting depths, 20-23
planting zones map, 76-77
poeticus narcissi, 69
powdery mildew, 33
Princess Irene tulips, 72
puschkinia (*Puschkinia scilloides*), 70

R

ranunculus (*Ranunculus asiaticus*), 70
reticulata iris, 63
rhizomes
   described, 8
   dividing, 37
rodents, 33
rotten bulbs, 25

S

Scilla species, 71
shrubs, 18
Siberian iris, 63
size (bulb), 24
slugs, 33
snails, 33
snowdrop (*Galanthus* species), 70
snowflake (*Leucojum* species), 71
soil preparation, 26-27
Sparaxis tricolor, 61

species lilies, 65
species narcissi, 69
species tulips, 73
spider lily (*Lycoris* species), 71
split-corona hybrids, 69
spring-blooming bulbs, 15
spring star flower (*Ipheion uniflorum*), 71
spuria iris, 63
squill (*Scilla* species), 71
staking bulbs, 31
sternbergia (*Sternbergia lutea*), 74
summer-blooming bulbs, 15
superphosphate, 27, 29

T

Tazetta hybrids, 69
tender bulbs
   cold factor and, 12-13
   storing, 35
thrips, 33
tiger flower, Mexican shell flower (*Tigridia pavonia*), 74
Triandrus hybrids, 69
Triteleia species, 56
Tritonia species, 59
true bulbs
   described, 8
   dividing, 37
trumpet narcissi, 69
tuberous begonia (*Begonia* x *tuberhybrida*), 74
tuberous roots
   described, 8
   dividing, 37
tubers
   described, 9
   dividing, 37
Tulipa fosteriana, 73
Tulipa kaufmanniana, 73
Tulipa species, 72-73
Tulipa turkestana, 73
Tulips, 72-73

V

viruses, 33

W

watering, 31
watsonia, bugle lily (*Watsonia* species), 75
weeding, 30
windflower (*Anemone blanda, Anemone coronaria*), 75
winter aconite (*Eranthis hyemalis*), 75
winter-blooming bulbs, 15

Z

Zantadeschia aethiopica, 57
zephyr flower, fairy lily (*Zephyranthes* species), 75

A NOTE FROM NK LAWN & GARDEN CO.

For more than 100 years, since its founding in Minneapolis, Minnesota, NK Lawn & Garden has provided gardeners with the finest quality seed and other garden products.

We doubt that our leaders, Jesse E. Northrup and Preston King, would recognize their seed company today, but gardeners everywhere in the United States still rely on NK Lawn & Garden's knowledge and experience at planting time.

We are pleased to be able to share this practical experience with you through this ongoing series of easy-to-use gardening books.

Here you'll find hundreds of years of gardening experience distilled into easy-to-understand text and step-by-step pictures. Every popular gardening subject is included.

As you use the information in these books, we hope you'll also try our lawn and garden products. They're available at your local garden retailer.

There's nothing more satisfying than a successful, beautiful garden. There's something special about the color of blooming flowers and the flavor of home-grown garden vegetables.

We understand how special you feel about growing things—and NK Lawn & Garden feels the same way, too. After all, we've been a friend to gardeners everywhere since 1884.